Original title:
The Quiet Space of Home

Copyright © 2025 Creative Arts Management OÜ
All rights reserved.

Author: Jameson Hartfield
ISBN HARDBACK: 978-1-80587-172-9
ISBN PAPERBACK: 978-1-80587-642-7

Moments of Tender Stillness

In the corner, socks do hide,
Peeking out, they take a ride.
Dust bunnies dance in a row,
Chasing the cat, what a show!

The fridge hums a friendly tune,
While spoons and forks form a cartoon.
Pizza boxes in a stack,
Napkin origami, that's a knack!

The shower sings a slippery song,
Rubber ducky joins along.
You never know when chaos lands,
With shampoo fights and bubble strands!

In this nook where laughter sweeps,
Every object has its peeps.
Living here is quite the jest,
Finding joy in every quest!

Breaths of Morning Gentle

Morning light spills across the floor,
Coffee brews, oh, sweet encore!
Socks mismatched, a sock puppet show,
Dance with the cat, her tail in tow.

Toast pops up like a jack-in-the-box,
Spreading jam that sticks like socks.
A rogue crumb finds its way to my nose,
Tickling laughter as breakfast glows.

A Universe Built in Brick and Beam

Walls are speakers for the crew,
Echoing laughter, old and new.
The ceiling fan does a whirl and spin,
Catching dust bunnies, let the games begin!

The fridge is a treasure, a cold, loud friend,
Its hum a tune that will never end.
Leftovers plotting their make-believe,
A taco wears a sombrero, oh, I believe!

Treasures in the Attic Light

In the attic, boxes stacked so high,
A hat that's older than the sky.
Nostalgia rides on the dust's soft breath,
A pirate's map to forgotten depth.

Old dolls gossip, knitting tales of yore,
Each story spills out, can't ignore.
A rubber chicken raises eyebrows right,
Oh, the treasures that dance in the light!

The Embrace of Familiar Space

Couch cushions whisper of deep, warm dreams,
Spilling secrets, or so it seems.
Remote controls, a band of their own,
Changing channels like kings on a throne.

Walls adorned with pictures, goofy grins,
A family portrait, where the chaos begins.
Every corner tells a joke or two,
In this haven, we laugh, and so we grew.

Hearthside Reverie

In winter, we nest like mice,
With snacks piled high, oh what a slice!
The cat steals crumbs and knocks things down,
While we wear laughter like a crown.

The fireplace crackles, sparks a dance,
As we take turns, and play our chance.
With marshmallows flying, oh what a sight,
Even the dog joins in our delight!

The Comfort of Closed Doors

Behind these doors, chaos may reign,
But with a snack, I'm never in pain.
TV blares, the kids do shout,
In my fortress, I don't have to scout.

Mom's secret stash of sweets divine,
With chocolate bars, I'll do just fine.
I lock the world and sip my tea,
While the rest of them just let it be!

A Haven in the Chaos

When life gets loud and all askew,
I turn the volume down, just for a view.
With pillows piled, like clouds in flight,
This messy truth feels so just right.

The cluttered floor is where I thrive,
With toys and socks, it feels alive.
A smudge of jam on my cheek, oh dear!
Yet here, my joy is crystal clear!

Memories in the Mellow Light

The lamps flicker like stars at night,
Casting warm glow, a cozy sight.
We gather 'round with tales to spin,
In laughter's embrace, let joy begin.

Old socks and slippers, a bond so tight,
In quirky outfits, we feel so right.
With every jest, our hearts take flight,
In this odd comfort, life's pure delight!

The Hush Between Walls

In corners where dust bunnies dance,
Old chairs creak with a funny stance.
A cat stares down from the highest shelf,
Thinking she's royalty, all by herself.

The fridge hums jokes to the tired light,
While socks plot adventures in the night.
An echo of laughter spills from a room,
A mystery hamster in search of its bloom.

Tranquil Corners of Memory

Under the table, socks have a feud,
While grandma's cookies simply ooze food.
Pictures whisper secrets of days old,
Of how dad once danced, or so he's told.

The clock ticks stories of time quite absurd,
Like a turtle who flew, or so we've heard.
Amidst the pillows, giggles take flight,
As shadows play hide and seek, oh what a sight!

The Warmth of Unspoken Love

In the kitchen, pots sing a tune,
While the toaster pops up like a jack-in-the-moon.
Coffee brews tales of sleepy-eyed glee,
As the sugar jar snickers, 'Just wait and see!'

The couch cushions plot a blanket invasion,
As remote controls make a grand persuasion.
Each glance and grin, a sweet, subtle game,
In this house of love, nothing feels the same.

Forgotten Pages of Lived Stories

Books stacked high in a teetering tower,
Each spine a witness to life's silly hour.
Dust motes twirl like ballerinas, so bright,
As a dog chases dreams, barking at night.

Crumbs of laughter fall from the seats,
Echoes of stories that time never beats.
In the attic, a hat with adventures galore,
Winks at those memories we couldn't ignore.

Neighbors of Silence and Sound

In the stillness, socks do flee,
Missing shoes greet me with glee.
The fridge hums a secret tune,
While cats plot chaos by the moon.

A creaky floor, an unspoken joke,
The toaster's pop is our morning poke.
Laughter hides in the cupboard's dark,
As the kettle's whistle sings 'let's spark.'

Half-Whispered Secrets

Behind closed doors, gossip reigns,
A dog's bark interrupts, yet remains.
The teapot spills tales of old,
While spoons clank like voices bold.

In corners, mischief remains unsaid,
Like the sock monster who likely fled.
With every laugh, a wrinkle appears,
In memories spun through the years.

Where Moments Collect in Dust

Dust bunnies roam, like little pets,
Each one tells stories that no one forgets.
Under the couch, lost treasures hide,
Like pizza slices out of pride.

Vacation photos stacked high and proud,
Each frame whispers, 'I was too loud!'
Coffee cups lined like soldiers in row,
Holding tales of chaos we know.

The Unsaid Words of Loved Ones

In the attic, memories prance,
Unspoken words in a wild dance.
Grandpa's chair creaks with tales of yore,
While Auntie's casserole's hard to ignore.

Beneath the laughter, a sigh does linger,
As pets steal socks with stealthy finger.
A chuckle escapes into the night,
Home's oddities hold love so tight.

Walls That Hold Our Stories

These walls can hear the silence laugh,
They share the tales of our mischief path.
Like that time the cat stole a sock,
And we laughed like it was a grand clock.

Faint echoes of the jokes we told,
While dodging crumbs that never got old.
The pasta-sauce splatter, a badge of pride,
A canvas where our chaos can't hide.

Full Cups and Empty Chairs

The cups are brimming with wild dreams,
While chairs hold secrets and giggles in seams.
We joke about the socks without a mate,
And wonder how we've come to this fate.

A cozy corner where socks disappear,
It's clear we've lost not just a pair.
But laughter spills from the table spread,
As we toast to fables that dance in our heads.

A Gallery of Memories Untouched

Dusty frames line up with glee,
Grinning portraits of a wild spree.
The photocopies from year gone past,
Were meant for framing, but they've been cast.

Each smile a clue to our greatest prank,
Like that time we made a time capsule tank.
Packed with dreams that are now quite silly,
Our gallery of laughter that hovers so frilly.

The Aroma of Peace

Spices dance like whispers in the air,
As we bounce around without a care.
The cookies laughing, the bread rhymes,
Even the kettle sings joyous chimes.

The smell of muffins and the coffee hum,
Entice us all like a rising sun.
In a world of notes, our home's the best,
With every savor, we're truly blessed.

A Canvas of Everyday Whimsy

In the kitchen, pots dance cheek to cheek,
While the kettle sings loud, a hilarious sneak.
Spatulas wave, in a wild kitchen jam,
As flour puffs up like a cloud with a slam.

Cushions collide in a cozy, soft fight,
The remote's missing, oh, what a delight!
Cats tumble over, plotting their next leap,
As we giggle, the laughter runs deep.

Corner Nooks and Cranny Comforts

In the corner, dust bunnies hold a ball,
While mismatched socks form a confetti wall.
A chair's got a squeak, joining the fun,
As the dog snores loudly, thinks he's number one.

Books stacked high, like a tower of dreams,
Each story spills out, puncturing the seams.
A tiny plant waves, needing a drink,
While we sip our tea and share a wink.

The Heartbeat of a Fire

The fireplace crackles, a playful jest,
With logs doing somersaults, oh what a fest!
Marshmallows laugh as they melt with glee,
While shadows dance wildly, just wait and see.

An old chair grumbles, it's telling a tale,
Of socks that went missing, of socks that went pale.
The cat joins in with a purr and a stretch,
As we giggle together, a moment to sketch.

Shadows Cradling the Night

As night falls softly, shadows play peek-a-boo,
A ghost in the corner, or could it be you?
The fridge hums a tune, a lullaby sweet,
While crickets applaud with a rhythmic repeat.

Blankets curled up, a cozy embrace,
Finds popcorn on cushions, what a messy place!
The clock ticks away, a tickle and tease,
In this delightful chaos, we find our ease.

Abode of Unraveled Thoughts

In corners, socks play hide and seek,
The cat's a thief, my lunch? At peak!
The dishes pile like wedding guests,
In chaos sweet, my heart finds rest.

A table set for one or six,
Why do forks know all the tricks?
The fridge hums tunes, an empty tune,
We dance with snacks beneath the moon.

Dust bunnies plot like secret spies,
They organize mock parties, no lies,
I find their trails where they convene,
In laughter, chaos reigns supreme.

Within these walls, the clock runs slow,
With every tick, the giggles grow,
And here, where silence sings its song,
I know I always do belong.

Serenity in the Swaying Curtains

Curtains flap like sails on seas,
They nod while I sip herbal teas,
The sun peeks in, and there's a grin,
While socks are lost where dreams begin.

The rug's a map of crumbs and cheer,
Adventures shared with snacks quite near,
Each footprint tells a story sweet,
In this domain, the laughs repeat.

Dust motes dance like they're on stage,
They twirl around, unfurl their age,
And every chair's a comfy throne,
While pillows hum a welcome tone.

Outside's a world, a bustling show,
But here, our laughter's the main flow,
In cozy corners, life's a dream,
Where silly antics reign supreme.

The Pulse of Evening Stillness

Evening falls, the cats conspire,
To steal my spot, how they conspire!
The couch, a sea of blankets tossed,
In this retreat, no love is lost.

The fridge hums softly, a lullaby,
It's full of treats, I can't deny,
As shadows stretch and giggles rise,
The clock begins to roll its eyes.

Each creak and groan sings tales untold,
Of waffles burned and laughter bold,
The popcorn's popped, the movies play,
In this domain, we drift away.

Time meanders, slipping through,
In every corner, joy is true,
And here amidst the fading light,
We find our peace, our hearts take flight.

Shelters of Kindred Spirits

In this abode where laughter rings,
The laundry sings of mismatched flings,
A fortress built of cushions stacked,
With snacks aplenty, we're so well-packed.

The odd sock tells a life of strife,
My kitchen's just a Baker's life,
While secrets swirl like air-fried fries,
And friendship always multiplies.

Underneath the coffee stains,
Lie notes of joy and silly pains,
We craft our tales through ebb and flow,
In every glance, we truly know.

So let us gather with a cheer,
In these four walls, our hearts appear,
Where every quirk has found a home,
And love surrounds when we may roam.

Where Dust Settles in Peace

In corners a spider spins her plans,
We make our peace with dust-bunny clans.
The couch is a throne of old snack remains,
Here laughter is louder, despite all the stains.

The cat stalks shadows with comedic flair,
Once sleek as a panther, now fluffy with care.
Each creak of the floor tells tales of the past,
While the fridge hums a tune, a laugh unsurpassed.

The coffee spills cheer on a poor worn-out rug,
The dog strikes a pose, a true perfect mug.
A world of odd treasures is just 'round the bend,
Where chaos and giggles blend without end.

Refuge Beneath the Roof

Underneath this roof, our circus begins,
The cat's on the table, the dog's wearing fins.
Mom's mixing potions for dinner tonight,
While Dad's in the corner, trying to write.

Grandma's knitting sweaters with holes that are grand,
And she swears it's fashion - we just nod in the stand.
We dance through the kitchen, dodging the stew,
As mysterious smells join the playful debut.

A meeting of wits as the laundry spins tales,
With socks in a battle, the lost one prevails.
Here secrets spill out, like jelly from jars,
While we chuckle and chatter, our own little stars.

Memories in a Dusty Frame

Old photos align with their faded charm,
Each face dressed in laughter, so soft and warm.
Grandpa's wild hair in a 70's dance,
As we giggle and ponder his questionable pants.

A frame of good times hangs just askew,
Like our family game nights, where none ever knew,
Who wins or who loses, it's all just for fun,
Arguments over rules always laughter won.

When life plays its tricks, we harness the fun,
Board games and cards bring us closer, not shun.
Our living room echoes with joy and delight,
In shadows of memories, we sparkle so bright.

Emblems of Safe Returns

The door swings wide, with a squeaky good cheer,
In comes the dog, his tail as a spear.
The shoes at the mat tell tales of the sun,
As we gather like squirrels, all cozy and fun.

Each coat hung just right for the battles they fight,
With pockets of treasures, collected in flight.
We swap all our stories over warm pots of tea,
And gather around for good food, you see.

Our home is a workshop where dreams take their form,
With inside jokes that keep us all warm.
Through trials and laughter, we find our own way,
Home is a haven, come what may.

A Symphony of Unheard Sounds

In kitchens where pots clatter loud,
And spoons dance a goofy jig,
The laughter echoes off the walls,
Like a symphony played by a pig.

The cat meows a rhythmic tune,
As the fridge hums a steady beat,
Footsteps shuffle from room to room,
Tailors the rhythm of our feet.

The clock ticks away with sass,
Counting moments of each day,
While socks bicker in the drawer,
In their playful, mismatched way.

Together we create a score,
Of silly quirks and joyful fun,
In this concert of unseen tunes,
Where the ruckus has just begun.

Aura of Familiar Shadows

In the corners, shadows dance,
Whispering secrets of the past,
They spin in their cozy trance,
Making memories stick and last.

An old chair creaks with delight,
As it shares a spunky snore,
The tablecloth holds a fight,
Between crumbs and tales of yore.

In every nook, a ghost or two,
Tiles hide the laughter shared,
Their antics bring a funny view,
Of a life that's boldly dared.

With echoes of our daily strife,
And comic moments intertwined,
These fleeting shapes become our life,
A comedy forever signed.

The Comfort of Old Socks

In a drawer, mismatched delight,
Each sock tells a tale of fun,
One has stripes, the other spots,
Fashion faux pas? Still number one!

Worn and tattered, they're a team,
Squishy pals that never stray,
They cozy up in the morning light,
Starting the day in a goofy way.

A right sock, a left sock, what a pair,
They slip and slide with a playful stand,
Together they tackle the day with flair,
Like a two-man band in a sockland.

So here's to those cozy feet,
Silly and warm in their dance,
In this world, it can't be beat,
The joy of a sock's romance.

A Portrait of Unseen Bonds

A family portrait on the wall,
With goofy smiles and silly poses,
Captured moments, giggles all,
As love blooms like garden roses.

Fumbling hands and laughing eyes,
The memories framed with haste,
Each click a moment, oh what a prize,
Creating a picture we can't waste.

In every glance, a story shared,
In jokes and whispers, bonds revealed,
While dog snores in the background bared,
A canvas of laughter, life concealed.

Together we weave this vibrant thread,
In colors bold and shades of gray,
In our hearts, where laughter's spread,
An unseen bond that brightens the day.

Whispers in the Hallway

In the hallway, I hear a squeak,
Is it a ghost, or just my cheek?
The dust bunnies dance, oh what a scene,
While my socks plot mischief, if you know what I mean.

The fridge hums tales of late-night snacks,
It whispers secrets when no one laughs.
The chairs are gossips, they squeak and creak,
In our silly kingdom, we play hide and seek.

Rug's a trampoline for the cat's great leaps,
As I dodge scattered toys, I'm in for keeps.
Every room has quirks, each corner has fun,
Life's a comedy here, never done!

Laughter echoes like a symphony's thread,
While we chase shadows until we're in bed.
Home's a circus, and we're all the show,
With giggles and grins, our hearts overflow.

Echoes of Familiar Rooms

In the living room, a blanket fight,
Pillows launch fast, what a silly sight!
The TV's blaring, but we hear it not,
As laughter erupts like a bubbling pot.

The kitchen brews chaos with pots and pans,
I dance with the spatula, oh, what a romance!
Cookies are sneaking off the counter's edge,
While I find my footing on a piggy bank's ledge.

In the bathroom, rubber ducks float with pride,
Splashing and laughing, they won't go hide.
The mirror reflects our silly grimaces,
As we strike a pose in the weirdest places.

Every room holds a twist, a tickle, a tease,
In the echo of home, let laughter please.
With every corner, a story unfolds,
In this playful realm, joy never grows old.

Secrets Beneath the Stairs

Under the stairs, what treasures abound?
A box of lost shoes and a really weird sound.
But beware the dust bunnies, they guard their haul,
As I tiptoe carefully, they loom quite tall.

Old board games whisper, 'Pick me up, play!'
Hidden beneath clutter, they beg for a day.
Forgotten socks peek out with a smirk,
As I unravel the mess, invoking a quirk.

Once in a while, a shoe may fall loose,
It lands with a thud—oh, such a truce!
High on the shelf, a teddy bears snooze,
Dreaming of adventures too fun to refuse.

Secrets hide here, in shadows so deep,
With laughter, we venture, no need for sleep.
In the space of our home, treasures never tire,
As we uncover stories that never expire.

Shadows of Solitude

In the quiet corners, shadows creep,
But in their stillness, I find a peep.
They wiggle and jiggle with the light's gentle sway,
As I giggle softly, they invite me to play.

The candlestick grins with a flickering flame,
Creating a dance that's hardly the same.
With each unique shadow, a figure appears,
A waltz of the weird, to invite all our cheers.

Outside the window, the trees sway and spin,
Casting odd shapes on the walls of my skin.
The clock dings a joke, too loud for the night,
While I giggle beneath its keeping delight.

So here in my corner, where shadows take form,
A cozy ruckus, where ideas warm.
Home's playful glee, in solitude's guise,
A mysterious chuckle, beneath starlit skies.

Portraits of Peace

In slippers soft, we prance like bears,
With cereal fights and wild hair flares.
Walls decorated with crayon art,
Our living room's a work of heart.

A pet cat stares with a judging glare,
While we pretend that we don't care.
Laundry piles like small mountains grow,
Each sock a mystery, where'd it go?

We dance in the kitchen, not a care in sight,
Bumping into walls, oh, what a fright!
We laugh so hard that the neighbors glare,
But in this madness, we feel laid bare.

Each little mess tells a tale of cheer,
In bursts of laughter, we draw near.
A gallery of joy, a shrine to fun,
With every quirk, we are forever one.

Where Time Stands Still

The clock ticks slowly, what a trick,
Time seems to laugh, oh, how quick!
We lounge in pajamas, living the dream,
Coffee spills tell tales, or so it seems.

Waking up late? What a glorious sin!
Finding last week's pizza stuck on your chin.
We say 'five more minutes,' but that's just a jest,
Who needs a schedule when we're so blessed?

The fridge hums melodies of frozen delight,
Leftovers whisper 'eat me' at night.
With every snack, we embrace the thrill,
In this timeless bubble, we've discovered our fill.

On couches, we ponder, with snacks piled high,
To sweep all the mess? Oh, let it fly!
In moments like these, we're young and we're free,
From the specter of time, we're too spry to flee.

Nestled in Rest

Blankets like clouds, soft and so warm,
Together we snuggle through any storm.
With popcorn kernels and witty exchanges,
Silly movies lead to laughter ranges.

Naps on the couch can feel like a throne,
Dreaming of worlds where we've never flown.
Waking up startled, what day is it now?
Time stands still as we make our vow.

Messy hair and sleepy grins,
The fun of the night still lingers within.
With cushions piled high like mountain peaks,
No judgment here, just friendly shrieks.

In cozy corners of joy we delight,
Cuddled together in the soft twilight.
Home wrapped in laughter and warmth of love,
The best kind of rest fit for stars above.

Threads of Togetherness

In matching socks of colors so bright,
We weave our tales from morning to night.
Craft projects gone awry, a paint spill here,
Together in chaos, we hold the dear.

Like tangled yarn in a cat's keen paw,
Life shreds our plan, yet leaves us in awe.
Each thread entwined, like stories we spin,
In this delightful mess, where do we begin?

Tangled on sofas, we puzzle and play,
Creating magic in our own silly way.
We share whimsical snacks, a feast fit for clowns,
In laughter and joy, we'll never wear frowns.

Together we dance in mismatched shoes,
In this wacky wonderland, we can't lose.
With every odd moment, a bond keeps us strong,
In threads of connection, we joyously belong.

A Labyrinth of Memories and Mirth

Beneath the sofa, lost my shoe,
A cat grabbed it, what could I do?
In hallways echo, voices play,
Ghosts of laughter come out to stay.

The fridge hums tunes, a serenade,
While dancing socks, a grand parade.
In corners sit, the books ask why,
Their secret tales, they can't deny.

With every bump, the ceiling creaks,
Ticklish moments, it's laughter that peaks.
A juggling act, my cup and tea,
In this home, chaos feels so free.

Time's a jester, wearing a grin,
As I step outside, I tumble in.
With every misstep, stories unfold,
Mirth dances brightly, never grows old.

Handprints on the Walls of Time

The walls bear marks of tiny hands,
Like modern art in wobbly strands.
Each smudge a tale, each stain a laugh,
The fingerprints chart our crazy path.

When the dog sneezes, we all jump high,
A game of charades with the world passing by.
In this house, every corner's alive,
With quirky secrets that always thrive.

The fridge notes whisper, "Can we eat?"
Beneath the table, our dog's tiny feet.
The world outside may spin and swirl,
But here inside, life's a merry whirl.

Memories bubble as the kettle sings,
In this silly kingdom, joy wears wings.
With every splash from the tub, we thrive,
Our twisted tales keep us all alive.

Warmth of the Twilight Glow

The sunset spills like grape juice sweet,
While chaos reigns near my two left feet.
Crayons scatter like confetti bright,
And crayons' yours? They're clearly a fight.

As shadows lengthen, the cat steals the chair,
While kids throw pillows, a cushy affair.
The clocks chuckle, they slow their pace,
For in this glow, there's just space for grace.

The air is thick with popcorn dreams,
And giggles echo in soft moonbeams.
The couch transforms into a magic ride,
With cuddly beasts on a fanciful slide.

In laughter's arms, the day softly goes,
As sleepyheads strike their last comic pose.
In the cozy cranny, dreams will flow,
A place where silliness feels like home.

The Echo After a Laugh

After the giggles, silence will creep,
Like a sneaky cat plotting its leap.
But oh! The echoes bounce off the wall,
A raucous past that still feels so tall.

Jokes from the dinner table sneak,
Like breadcrumbs we leave when we speak.
Every grin hangs like a chandelier,
Reflecting humor, both far and near.

The dog rolls over, an audience sweet,
To our antics, he can't help but compete.
His furry nose hits the floor with a thud,
What follows next? A blanket of mud!

Quiet moments hide behind our sighs,
Yet in this stillness, laughter never dies.
It lingers softly, a memorable song,
In the midst of peace, we carry along.

Soft Corners of My World

In the nook where the socks go,
Lost forever, a cheeky foe.
The cat sprawls wide, taking claims,
While I search for a pair of games.

Books stacked high like a tower brave,
Each novel whispers, 'Please, just save.'
I trip on a shoe, it laughs and grins,
It's always chaos where comfort begins.

Leftover snacks hold secret names,
In my fridge, they play silly games.
Mismatched dishes hold yesterday's stew,
It's gourmet doubt, but I still chew.

Here's a quilt covered in cat hair,
A masterpiece of love and despair.
In this charming mess, life feels bright,
The soft corners make wrongs feel right.

Sanctuary of Silence

Walls that hold whispers of laughter,
Echo the noises that come after.
The toaster explodes, a breakfast thrill,
While I search for coffee, time to kill.

Dishes piled high, a tower of fun,
Mount Dishmore, conquer? I just run!
The clock ticks louder, mocking my pace,
In this chaos is my favorite place.

The couch is a monster, a vacuum's beast,
It swallows my remote, a bedtime feast.
Pajamas are armor for a warrior's night,
Defending the cushions till morning's light.

Outside the world is a whirlwind rush,
Inside I bask in joy's gentle hush.
Every corner treasures a story or two,
In this quiet chaos, I find my crew.

The Embrace of Familiarity

A rug that squeaks when I take a step,
Saying hello with its soft little rep.
The fridge hums a tune I know by heart,
It's a solo concert, my favorite part.

Neighbors chatter like a morning show,
While I pretend I'm fine — but no one knows.
Each creaky floorboard tells tales untold,
They've witnessed laughter, they've seen the bold.

The dog's in charge, with a crucial role,
Guarding the house like a fluffy patrol.
He snags my lunch, gives me a wink,
In this uproar, I just can't think.

With mismatched chairs and quirky looks,
This is my realm, away from the books.
A place where strange feels perfectly right,
In the warmth of oddities, I find delight.

Tranquility Among the Walls

Under the blanket, TV's my guide,
Remote control knight, couch is my ride.
The popcorn pops, it dances in glee,
As I root for villains, they root for me!

Candles are flickering, doing their thing,
Scented like cookies, a sweet little fling.
But when I burn toast, the smoke's like a crow,
An air freshener, here we go!

Pillows piled high, a fortress of fluff,
I dive in deep, because life's kinda rough.
Each cushion sighs with a giggling sound,
In this softness, my joy is found.

So let the dishes and laundry stack high,
As laughter and warmth embrace the sly.
In these lively walls, I find my fame,
A never-ending show, and I'm the same!

Windows to the Everyday

Through the glass, the cat does stare,
Watching squirrels without a care.
Muffin crumbs dance on the floor,
While my slippers beg for more!

Mailman brings the daily news,
Pajamas still my happy shoes.
Neighbors gossip on the street,
While I sip my tea, so sweet!

Potatoes boil, send a huff,
Burnt toast makes the munching tough.
Laughter echoes from the halls,
As I dodge the bouncing balls!

From these panes, life's antics frame,
Our world's a hilarious game!
Every moment, a new delight,
In this home, my heart takes flight!

An Invitation to Repose

Couch cushions, a fort built high,
Penguin plushes stick nearby.
TV bings, a show's long pause,
Time to snooze without a cause!

Blankets pile, oh, what a sight,
Afternoon fades into night.
Remote controls are my best pals,
Binge-watching while the world howls!

Cookies crumble on my chest,
Does this sofa know the rest?
Fridge gives whispers of delight,
Non-stop munching feels so right!

As I sink into this pit,
Life's a laugh, and I won't quit!
Here's the invitation's tone,
"Stay awhile; you're not alone!"

Anchor of the Familiar

Old shoes lined near the door,
Family laughter echoes more.
Fridge magnets dance with cheer,
Bringing quirks that feel so dear!

Dust bunnies under the chair,
Wonder if they have a fair?
Chasing socks is a must-do,
Who knew laundry hid so many blues!

Plants grow tall, or so they claim,
With names that seem quite lame.
"Fido" for the tallest fern,
And "Gertrude" makes me laugh and churn!

This is love wrapped up in glee,
An anchor in the absurd spree.
Every corner holds a dance,
In this chaos, I find my chance!

Pillows Embraced by a Dream

In this nest, my thoughts drift far,
When I dream, I'm a rock star!
Pillow fights with jolly glee,
These little clouds are home to me!

Beneath the stars, the night ignites,
Funny monsters join my flights.
Cereal bowls hold strange lore,
As I munch, they implore more!

Slumber parties with teddy bears,
Frightened dreams and laugh-filled scares.
Snuggles warm, a perfect scene,
In this land, I reign supreme!

So here I lie, with heart so light,
Each silly thought, a pure delight.
Dreams are born where comfort screams,
In this world of soft, sweet dreams!

Echoes of Laughter Past

In the corner, a sock on the wall,
Cat's favorite toy, the dog takes the fall.
Dishes stacked like a crooked tower,
Each giggle brings back that silly hour.

Grandma's stories, a fun little tease,
About awkward dates and a strong vermin sneeze.
A dance in the kitchen with mismatched shoes,
Spilling the flour, oh, what a ruse!

The knock-knock jokes that never get old,
Mixed with the warmth that this house can hold.
Funny faces in the mirror reflect,
Here's to the laughter we never neglect.

As night falls, we share tales anew,
Of a missing spoon and the time we flew.
With every echo, a memory to cast,
We cradle the joy, the party that lasts.

A Place Between Dreams

Blankets piled high, a fort made with flair,
Two kids, one cat, a snack—or a scare?
Imagined battles in pillowcase night,
The general's decree: It's time for a bite!

Chocolate crumbs lead to a hushed retreat,
Sneaking in brownies, a tasty deceit.
A tickle attack, giggles explode,
In this wacky world, we lighten the load.

The ghosts of our bedtime mischief arise,
As shadows dance in the ceiling's disguise.
We fight just to stay awake for the show,
As sleep steals the stage, we whisper, "Oh no!"

In the space between dreams, we find our delight,
Trading secrets till dawn's early light.
With a chuckle and snore, the night drifts away,
Leaving laughter to brighten our day.

The Melody of Togetherness

In the kitchen, chaos plays like a song,
Spaghetti flinging, nothing feels wrong.
Mom waltzes by with a sauce-splashing grin,
While Dad stirs the pot, his dance moves begin.

The fridge hums a tune of forgotten snacks,
While we try to remember where the side dish packs.
As forks hit the plates, it's a clattering band,
Each bite a note, nothing bland in our hands.

The clink of the glass, cheers fill the space,
As laughter erupts, lighting up every face.
Funny stories weave through the breadcrumbs of time,
In this grand symphony, we sing in our rhyme.

With each passing meal, our hearts intertwine,
Sharing mishaps with a sprinkling of shine.
Together we dance, in this life's grand ballet,
A melody of moments that never fade away.

Frames of Forgotten Times

Dusty frames hang, a time capsule sighs,
Of dad's epic pants from the 90s surprise.
Photos of moments all frozen in glee,
Check out the hair—how wild could it be?

The toddler in pink, with cake on her face,
Caught mid-sneeze at her first birthday race.
Grandpa's big grin, mismatched socks galore,
Each picture tells tales that we can't ignore.

We stumble through stories while laughter ignites,
Like Uncle Joe's dance moves on Christmas nights.
The framed memories blend with our cheerful wit,
Celebrating the chaos that makes us all fit.

So, here's to the frames that capture our zest,
For laughter and love are always the best.
In the gallery of hearts, we hang every smile,
Creating bright moments that stretch every mile.

The Stillness of an Open Door

A breeze sneaks in, makes curtains dance,
My cat leaps high, in a clumsy prance.
Dust motes floating, in the sun's bright glow,
Silent giggles from my toe-stubbing foe.

The dog sniffs loudly, a suspicious sound,
As neighbors gossip, they gather round.
I sip my tea, it's gone cold, oh dear,
I wave to the postman, he waves with cheer.

A sandwich waits, still on the plate,
While my lunch breaks forth, a laugh at fate.
The clock ticks softly, but time flies high,
In this open portal, I won't say goodbye.

A kiss from the breeze brings whispers and tales,
Of socks without partners and forgotten mails.
While chaos swirls, I simply adore,
My feet find comfort in the open door.

Retreat from the World Outside

Umbrella in hand, I dash to escape,
Yet I trip and twirl, oh, what a shape!
A pot of tea brews, my cozy delight,
As rain drums the roof in a comedic fight.

The cat looks at me, with paws crossed tight,
Like, "What's with the splashes? You're losing the fight!"

I chuckle aloud; the world's way too loud,
In my fortress of socks, I feel so proud.

The fridge hums softly, a strange serenade,
As leftovers plot, a culinary raid.
I dodge every wicked, week-old surprise,
With an apron on guard, I'm a chef in disguise.

So here I retreat, in my fortress of fun,
With pillows as shields, I'll weather the run.
The out there can wait, with its hurry and fuss,
In here, I am king, so just give me the bus!

Nestled Between Comforts

Cushions like clouds, I'm buried within,
Remote in hand, oh, where to begin?
With snacks piled high, a feast on my lap,
I'm a couch potato, caught in a trap.

The dog growls low, at squirrels on the screen,
While I nibble popcorn, what a lovely scene!
Socks on my feet, a mismatched affair,
But who can judge me in my snugged-up lair?

Pajamas are champions in this cozy realm,
Where chaos is snoozed, and I take the helm.
I slide on the floor, as I reach for the chips,
With dreams that involve large, exuberant skips.

So nestle beside me, in soft fabric waves,
We'll chuckle at sitcoms and how they misbehave.
In this padded castle, where laughter ignites,
We'll roll into giggles, our very own lights.

Soft Footsteps on Wooden Floors

Tiptoe through shadows, the floorboards creak,
As I search for the snack stash, oh, what a peek!
The dog follows closely, a partner in crime,
With matching excitement, we're masters of time.

Each squeaky floorboard, a story to tell,
Of dances at midnight and some pillow fights' swell.
We glide like whispers, through the dawn's golden light,
While breakfast becomes our delightful delight.

The cat gives a glare, from the top of the stairs,
With judgement, she sits, like she doesn't care.
But her tail gives a flick, as she ponders her role,
In our lazy escapades, we make quite the whole.

So here's to the moments, in the stillness we find,
With laughter and snacks, an adventure unlined.
For life's little quirks, we tiptoe with glee,
On wooden floors echoing, just you and me.

Lullabies of Everyday Life

The clock ticks loud, it's time for bed,
But snacks still linger, dancing in my head.
I close my eyes, but the fridge sings near,
A serenade to snacks, oh so dear.

Pajamas on, I gather my dreams,
A mountain of pillows, or so it seems.
The cat's in my lap, purring in rhyme,
And here comes the dog, demanding more time.

My bed's a vessel, a ship of my own,
Set sail on seas, where no one's alone.
Every creak in the floor brings giggles anew,
A funny little chorus, just for the crew.

So hush now, please, as I start to snore,
With laughter and snacks, who could ask for more?
In nightly adventures, I trust my heart,
For lullabies play, where the wild dreams start.

Beneath the Roof's Embrace

Under the ceiling, I dance with delight,
As dust bunnies pirouette in the light.
The couch is a throne, where champions sit,
With popcorn in hand, and no need to quit.

Mismatched socks, a fashion parade,
Each step a giggle, oh what a charade.
The dog joins in, with a wag and a spin,
It's a party of laughter, let the fun begin!

The walls are my stage, the floors are the dance,
To every silliness, I give my best chance.
With each painted corner, a story is spun,
Beneath this old roof, we gather as one.

So raise up a cheer for the chaos we keep,
In this quirky old haven, where memories leap.
Life's just more funny when it's shared far and wide,
Beneath the roof's embrace, we all take great pride.

The Palette of Warmth

In a world full of colors, I paint my way,
From cereal breakfasts to afternoon play.
Each hue brazen and bold, a brilliant sight,
Spaghetti sunsets and broccoli night.

The fridge holds a rainbow, a feast for the eyes,
A tapestry woven with savory ties.
But as I mix mustard with ketchup for fun,
I giggle at the masterpiece I've just begun.

Watercolors drip as I splash and I sing,
Crafting a canvas of everyday zing.
The laughter erupts, a splash here and there,
In this playful gallery, we all share.

So grab your brushes, let's blend and explore,
Each mess an adventure, who could ask for more?
With love as our palette, bright tales we weave,
In the art of our lives, we happily believe.

Safe Harbor of the Heart

With blankets piled high and snacks on the side,
In my fortress of cushions, I safely reside.
The world outside may be wild and loud,
But inside here, I'm whimsical and proud.

The fish in the tank, they wiggle and cheer,
As I share my secrets, hoping they hear.
The cat takes a leap, lands right in my lap,
In this cozy retreat, we take a long nap.

Beneath the soft glow of my favorite lamp,
I harbor the quirks, where nobody's a damp.
The walls whisper secrets, the floor holds the truth,
In my haven of laughter, I treasure my youth.

So join me, dear friends, in this joyful reprieve,
Where the heart finds a place it truly believes.
In this harbor of warmth, we build our own art,
It's the laughter and love that fill up this heart.

Embrace of Stillness

In the corner sits a cat, so wise,
He watches me with sleep-filled eyes.
The laundry piles up, like a small mound,
While he dreams of fish and chasing around.

The fridge hums softly with a moan,
While the dust bunnies claim their throne.
I trip over shoes which seem to conspire,
As I shuffle around, fueled by desire.

The couch is a kingdom, a well-earned rest,
With snacks hidden deep, I'm truly blessed.
I ponder the dishes, a mountain's view,
And wonder if they'll just wash themselves too!

In the stillness, laughter echoes clear,
As my sock puppets plot world domination here.
In this cozy chaos, I find my glee,
Each day a comedy, starring only me.

Hearth of Heartbeats

The kettle whistles, like a bird on cue,
While I search for cups, a scavenger too.
Tea spills gently over the rim,
As I juggle my thoughts—good luck, I whims!

The remote control is a treasure to find,
Living room chaos, a puzzle aligned.
Pillows are knights, guarding cushions so tight,
As I sink in, laugh at my own silly plight.

The oven timer shrieks like a siren at sea,
I dash to the kitchen—what did I decree?
A casserole bubbling, or maybe charred gold,
It's always a surprise, or so I'm told.

Between the giggles and stumbles each day,
Home wraps around me in its quirky way.
With heartbeats and laughter, nothing feels wrong,
In this hilarity, I find where I belong.

Nest of Forgotten Dreams

Beneath the stairs lie remnants of old,
A dusty collection of stories retold.
Forgotten toys whisper tales from the past,
As I wade through memories, the die is cast.

Old books peer out with their covers so worn,
Every page holds a dream, gently torn.
In this haunted nook, I'm swallowed in thought,
Did I really believe I could yodel a lot?

Laughter erupts from the cobwebbed space,
As squirrels try to join with their frantic race.
I chase dreams like butterflies drifting afar,
In the safety of clutter, I'm the true star.

With mismatched socks and crayons galore,
Here I'm an artist, what more could I score?
In the nest of nostalgia, I banter and scheme,
As laughter reverberates—life's sweetest dream.

Silent Echoes in the Room

The clock ticks loudly, counting my snacks,
Each tick a reminder of forgotten tracks.
Where did I leave that last mug of tea?
Oh, here's a sock—at least it's not me!

Walls hold whispers of stories to tell,
As I trip on the rug—a soft, fuzzy swell.
I'll blame the dust—yes, it danced with my feet,
Making my shuffle feel more like a feat.

In every corner, a giggle hides tight,
Behind the sofa, a dust bunny takes flight.
It leaps for the window, as if to declare,
That even stillness can't keep it from air!

With cushions as clouds, I float for a while,
Imagining dragons with cheeky smiles.
In this echoing silence, I find my delight,
Balancing fun, in my quirky home light.

Colors of Calm in a Fractured World

In the corner, a cat naps so slight,
While my worries take off in mid-flight.
The walls whisper tales painted bright,
As mismatched socks engage in a fight.

The kettle sings tunes, my favorite song,
While toasters conspire, it won't be long.
The fridge argues who's right or wrong,
In a household where chaos feels strong.

A rainbow of mess, each hue a delight,
A gathering of oddities, pure and polite.
In the game of mishaps, we all feel light,
And laughter erupts—what a comical sight!

Fragments of joy in this fractured place,
An ironic dialect, a familial grace.
Every day's a riddle, a funny embrace,
As we giggle and dance in this warm, cozy space.

Staircases of Memory

Each staircase creaks with laughter's sound,
Carrying my thoughts up and down.
With each step taken, odd sights abound,
Like grandma's old hat, such treasures found.

Descend for tea, the kettle's on fire,
Unruly thoughts that never tire.
The dog winks, as if he conspires,
To steal my biscuit—my sweet desire.

Climbing again, I ponder the past,
Where time never seems to move fast.
Old family photos, a charming blast,
Of outfits that surely weren't meant to last.

So many stories squeezed in each wall,
From silly antics to epic fall.
Step by step, we rise and recall,
A whole rollercoaster in a close hall.

The Dance of Dust Motes

In sunbeams where dust motes twirl and spin,
They waltz through the air, a whimsical fin.
Each one's a performer with a silly grin,
In a ballet of chaos, let the fun begin!

A sneeze disrupts their graceful show,
They scatter and gather as if they know.
Like tiny dancers caught in the flow,
Their giggles echo, "We're putting on a show!"

The bookshelves gasp as they twinkle bright,
All holding secrets wrapped up tight.
A tumble of yarn joins the line of sight,
As we sit back and delight in the sight.

With each little puff, they float and sway,
Our home becomes a stage for play.
In this grand performance, we laugh and stay,
Immersed in the charm of everyday.

Familial Threads of Love

Tangled threads in a grand tapestry,
Each loop a story of wild jubilee.
A sock on my head, oh what glee!
As family bonds weave together so free.

A parade of mismatched shoes at the door,
All lining up for their dance on the floor.
With laughter erupting like never before,
Every footstep, a new tale to explore.

Whiskers twitching in the afternoon sun,
The dog's got a plan—oh, what fun!
Chasing his tail, he thinks he's won,
While two cats watch, judging this run.

Come gather 'round, toss the towels together,
For goofy moments are always the tether.
In this crazy quilt, we're light as a feather,
Crafting a life that's as bright as the weather.

The Space Between Heartbeats

In the room where socks go missing,
A dance floor for lost dreams,
Every tick-tock takes a pause,
Like my cat in sunbeam beams.

The fridge hums a quirky tune,
While leftovers join the show,
A symphony of silly sounds,
In this one-bullet-time fiasco.

The couch keeps secrets, snug and tight,
As I trip over bits of fluff,
The hiccups of a lazy day,
We all laugh it off, that's enough.

Underneath the wooden beams,
Life whispers jokes, soft and spright,
A world built of giggles and cheer,
In a space just far from sight.

Breaths Stolen in Repose

Snores ripple like sweet thunder,
With pillows as my nearest crowd,
The dog leaves behind his scent,
As I'm smothered, head down, proud.

Teaspoon trumpets on the shelf,
Dance-offs in a cup of brew,
The kettle's waltz is funny stuff,
As I step on gum, who knew?

Inspirations come with crumbs,
Laughter lingers with the dust,
Each moment sways like a feather,
We float on giggles — that's a must.

In this whirlpool of cozy dreams,
The clock giggles, plays along,
While I trade a crust for a laugh,
In this realm where feasts belong.

Tapestries of Time Woven Here

Cook books spill their secrets wide,
As aprons play dress-up dress,
Ketchup and mustard take side bets,
On who'll make the bigger mess.

The clock grins, tipping on its face,
As I dance with a spatula in hand,
Every dish a nominee,
For the worst chef in the land.

Through windows framed with laughter,
The sun creeps in, a cheeky spy,
Pigeons perform their daily show,
As I wave back, oh me, oh my!

Here, time is a curious thread,
Tangled up in joy we weave,
With each wink from a passing cat,
Reminding us to just believe.

The Quiet of a Single Lightbulb

In the glow of a lone light source,
I predict a shadowy dance,
The lamp, my partner, winks at me,
As we twirl in a silly trance.

Moths audition for a fleeting role,
While I applaud with a light clap,
Caught in a spotlight of mischief,
As the bulb takes an unexpected nap.

Whispers echo off the walls,
As laundry flirts with the breeze,
Each sock a performer, bright and bold,
Seeking fame with perfect ease.

So here's to this dim-lit affair,
Where giggles glow and stir,
In the warmth of a lightbulb's cheer,
We find joy in the furry blur.

Garlands of Laughter and Tears

In my living room, socks are rarely paired,
Cats roll and tumble, with such flair;
Spilled snacks create a crunching floor,
Who needs a gym when you have this chore?

The fridge hums jokes, ice cream's a treat,
Dinner's a game of hide and seek;
When I burn the toast, I just give a grin,
"A new recipe!" I claim with a spin.

The couch becomes a stage at night,
As blankets turn to capes, what a sight;
Superpowers come in cheesy show,
With laughter echoing, our hearts aglow.

So in this chaos, we find our cheer,
The sound of giggles is what we hold dear;
With every sip of tea, we share a tale,
In this garland of fun, we always prevail.

The Still Pond of Daily Living

Mornings start with mismatched shoes,
Coffee spills, it's the best morning news;
The toaster pops, and we jump in fright,
Breakfast battles are pure delight.

Chores pretend to be a dreadful task,
But then I find that old Halloween mask;
It sparks a giggle and a dance around,
In mundane moments, joy can be found.

The garden whispers secrets in the breeze,
While weeds throw parties; they do as they please;
I talk to the plants, they talk back in sprout,
In this wild mismatch, what's there to doubt?

Each day's a riddle, laughter's the key,
Finding humor in agony is our decree;
In the gentle mess of everyday life,
We blossom and bloom, avoiding all strife.

Where Hearts Unfold

In the corners, dust bunnies play hide and seek,
While I trip over toys with a chuckle so meek;
The laundry basket says it's got a plan,
To fold itself, I don't know how it can.

These walls have witnessed both giggles and tears,
As I dance on the tile with joy and some fears;
Every crack's a joke that only we know,
Where secrets get lost in the laughter's flow.

Board games turn fierce as we scream and we cheer,
Dice rolling like thunder from every corner near;
When the cat snatches the knight, we cry, "Not again!"
In this realm of fun, we'll keep playing, amen.

So, gather 'round, with hearts open wide,
In the chaos of life, there's nothing to hide;
Here in our laughter, the world feels so bright,
Where our tales and our hearts can take flight.

Riddles in Long-forgotten Rooms

That closet hides monsters, or maybe just shoes,
Its door creaks a warning that leaves me confused;
Dust dances like fairies, enjoying the gloom,
As I laugh at the ghosts in this cluttered tomb.

Old memories linger like a half-eaten pie,
Each slice is a tale of both laughter and sighs;
Trinkets and treasures, forgotten and grand,
Tell stories of nights spent with joy at hand.

The attic's a spaceship, oh let's take a ride,
In boxes of chaos, lost dreams should abide;
We'll wear scarves like capes, explore every nook,
In a world of imagination, it's all in the book.

So let's twirl in the mess, while we take it all in,
Each riddle unraveled brings giggles akin;
In shadows and whispers, our laughter is bright,
As we discover the fun in the quirks of the night.

Solace in Routine

In pajamas I sit, a cereal king,
Slurping milk like a royal thing.
The cat looks on with judging eyes,
While I munch loudly, the cereal flies.

The same old show on every night,
Laugh tracks echo, such pure delight.
I dance in the kitchen to songs so cheesy,
My dog joins in, both of us easy.

I lay out my socks like a treasure map,
One is missing—it's such a trap.
With all the pillows, a fort I'll make,
Adventure awaits, for goodness' sake.

With each routine, a giggle unfolds,
In the mundane, humor's pure gold.
Finding joy in the simple grind,
This cozy chaos, so perfectly kind.

Beneath the Canopy of Care

Underneath the quilt, we hide away,
Google maps wronged us in grand display.
Popcorn battles and pillow fights,
My partner and I, such silly sights.

Plants in the corner, all wildly grown,
Talk to them often, they're never alone.
One just whispered, "You need some sun,"
I answered back, "You're not much fun!"

In the kitchen, I cook with flair,
One dish burns, but who wouldn't dare?
Laughter erupts as we taste and groan,
Is it a meal or an episode of 'grown'?

Beneath laughter, affection traces,
Where each mishap leaves funny faces.
Sharing the chaos, both silly and fair,
In this home, we're a whimsical pair.

Whispers in the Hallway

The hallway creaks with secret tales,
Of long-lost socks and forgottenails.
Ghosts of pizza slices past are found,
In this funny realm where crumbs abound.

I tiptoe past the echoing loo,
"Who left the toilet seat up? Was it you?"
A note on the fridge, a strange demand,
"Please stop dancing like you're in a band!"

The dust bunnies plot their great escape,
While I chase them down in my bathrobe cape.
With each corner turned, a giggle stirs,
As I lose to the vacuum, oh, the blurs!

These whispers linger, they fill the air,
In my home, mischief is everywhere.
So join the fun, don't you be shy,
Every laugh here, we'll amplify!

Shadows of Familiarity

In the shadowy kitchen, lights flicker bright,
A game of hide and seek each night.
The fridge hums softly, a secretive friend,
As we plot mischief around the bend.

I trip on my cat, nearly go splat,
While he lounges back like, "What's wrong with that?"
The dog yawns wide, a comical sight,
As he dreams of chasing, oh what a fright!

The laundry pile grows, a mountain so high,
Each shirt tells tales of days gone by.
"Is this a romper or an oversized mess?"
Even the clothes seem to jest and confess.

Shadows dance as the night unfolds,
In this cozy space, humor holds.
With each little quirk, we share our tune,
As laughter swells under the glowing moon.

Gentle Corners of Solitude

In a cozy nook, I sit and sigh,
With socks that clash, oh me, oh my!
A dust bunny rolls, my only friend,
In this snug corner, where troubles end.

The cat is sprawled, a furry lump,
I swear he plots, he's quite the chump!
He's got the space, I need a chair,
Guess I'll just sit on the floor right there.

A cup of tea, it's gone too cold,
Stories of old, they never get old.
Each sip a laugh, a giggle or two,
In my fancy fortress, where dreams come true.

And now I hear the fridge's hum,
Its witty jokes, they make me numb.
I wave to the plants, they wave right back,
In this little realm, I'm on the right track.

Soft Light Through the Window

Sunlight creeps on the kitchen floor,
An invitation to snack and explore.
I'm sneaking cookies, just one or three,
But I know the scales don't smile at me!

The curtains dance, a funny waltz,
While I pretend I can't hear my faults.
The dog looks up, with puppy eyes,
As if he knows my secret surprise.

Butterflies flit, outside they play,
While I'm stuck here, wasting the day.
"Where's my cake?" I dramatically moan,
Oh dear, the last slice is all but gone!

Yet in this light, I concoct a scheme,
To bake a pie, fulfill my dream.
Ingredients may scatter and fly,
But laughter erupts, oh my, oh my!

Echoes of Laughter Past

In the hall we shared so many smiles,
Where echoes linger, extending for miles.
The board games clash, a loud ruckus,
Each roll of dice brings more of us.

The tales that rise, and tumble and fall,
Of epic fails, we laugh through it all.
A spilt drink, a goofy dance,
In this memory lane, we take a chance.

Grandma's jokes, they age like wine,
Nudging us, "Where's that cake of mine?"
The cat looks on, with judging eyes,
In this home, there's no room for lies.

The walls may hear, but they won't tell,
Of all the laughter, it knows too well.
So let's raise a toast, to silly bliss,
In every corner, there's warmth, not a miss.

Sanctuary of Everyday Moments

In the chaos of breakfast, cereal flies,
Milk spills over, our laughter sighs.
A battle of spoons, who's got the last?
In these daily antics, we're free at last!

Dishes pile high, a tower of fun,
They wobble and jiggle, a balancing run.
I declare a truce, let's play pretend,
In this washing game, I'll be your friend!

Evenings close in, with hugs and snorts,
As laughter roams through our comfy forts.
The couch transforms to a spaceship bright,
Where dreams take off into the night.

With every moment of light and cheer,
This hub is the joy we hold so dear.
Where silly dances and smiles abound,
In our little world, pure fun is found.

The Breath of Stillness

In the corner, cat snores loud,
While I sit here, feeling proud.
The teapot whistles a tune so sweet,
But it's just my feet, that's hard to beat.

Chairs creak softly, a gentle joke,
As I ponder what's next to poke.
The tv flickers, a ghostly dance,
Is it horror or just my pants?

Mismatched socks, a fashion crime,
I wear them daily, never mind.
In this calm, my chaos looks fine,
Like a home where laughter intertwines.

So here I sit, in silly bliss,
With every laugh, I steal a kiss.
The world may rush, but here, I roam,
In my little patch, I find my home.

Reflections in the Windowpane

Each morning light brings a joke anew,
I brush my teeth while I dance for two.
The pancake flips, then hits the floor,
The dog just stares, demanding more.

The neighbor's cat gives me the eye,
It's plotting something, oh my, oh my!
I'll never know what's in its plans,
But it steals my sun and does a prance.

Dishes pile high, a towering feat,
They sing of neglect, a chorus sweet.
I promise to wash them, someday, maybe,
Right after my snack, if I'm not too shavy.

Outside, a squirrel with nuts to show,
Preparing for winter, the little pro.
Meanwhile I sit, a laugh in the air,
In my fortress of snack, without a care.

A Tapestry of Tranquil Moments

A patchwork quilt tucked on the chair,
With crumbs of cookies, and silly hair.
I sip my drink, watch the world slide by,
The dog looks up, as if to sigh.

The clock ticks loud, a comical beat,
Saying 'hurry up' to my constipation feat.
I argue back, in my sleepy haze,
Who says I'm late? I walk funny ways.

Plants whisper secrets, to each next door,
While I stumble about, always wanting more.
I trip on the rug, then burst into cheer,
A connoisseur of spills, it's my career!

So let laughter echo through these walls,
In this cozy haven, where the silly calls.
In every moment, a mischievous grin,
In this tapestry, let the fun begin!

The Language of Dusty Tomes

Books piled high, a teetering tower,
Each one smiles, with its own power.
They whisper tales of worlds long gone,
While dust bunnies cha-cha across the lawn.

I search for wisdom, it's quite a chore,
But find a sock, or maybe four.
Each page I turn, another chuckle here,
A twist of fate, a phantom sneer.

The coffee spills, a tragic splash,
As I chase wisdom in a mad dash.
But within these pages, a laugh I shall find,
A heart so light, a soul intertwined.

The stories linger, playfully tease,
Mixing in laughter, like a friendly breeze.
With crooked lines and joyful blooms,
In this library, laughter resumes!

www.ingramcontent.com/pod-product-compliance
Lightning Source LLC
Chambersburg PA
CBHW060115230426
43661CB00003B/197